A PHONE CALL FROM DALIAN

A PHONE CALL FROM DALIAN
来自大连的电话

Selected poetry of

Han Dong
韩东

Edited by Nicky Harman

Translated from Chinese by Nicky Harman,
Maghiel van Crevel, Yu Yan Chen,
Naikan Tao, Tony Prince & Michael Day

Zephyr Press & The Chinese University Press of Hong Kong
Brookline, Mass | Hong Kong

Chinese Copyright © 2012 by Han Dong
Foreword Copyright © 2012 by Nicky Harman
Introduction Copyright © 2012 by Maghiel van Crevel
English Translation Copyright © 2012 by Nicky Harman, Maghiel van Crevel,
Yu Yan Chen, Naikan Tao, Tony Prince & Michael Day

Cover image by Xu Bing
Book design by typeslowly
Printed in Hong Kong

This publication is supported by the Jintian Literary Foundation. Zephyr Press
also acknowledges with gratitude the financial support of the
Massachusetts Cultural Council.

masscultural council.org

Zephyr Press, a non-profit arts and education 501(c)(3) organization,
publishes literary titles that foster a deeper understanding of cultures
and languages. Zephyr Press books are distributed to the trade in the U.S.
and Canada by Consortium Book Sales and Distribution [www.cbsd.com]
and by Small Press Distribution [www.spdbooks.org].

Published for the rest of the world by:
The Chinese University Press
The Chinese University of Hong Kong
Sha Tin, N.T., Hong Kong

Cataloguing-in publication data is available from the Library of Congress.

ZEPHYR PRESS
www.zephyrpress.org

JINTIAN
www.jintian.net

THE CHINESE UNIVERSITY PRESS
www.chineseupress.com

CONTENTS

The Poetics of Disbelief

Maghiel van Crevel[*]

Since the 1980s, the modern Chinese poetry that has mattered—in China, and in the rest of the world —is often called "avant-garde," as distinct from "official" poetry associated with a politically sanctioned, orthodox literary establishment. Avant-garde poetry has overwhelmingly emerged through "underground" journals, privately produced and distributed outside state-controlled channels. The journals were spearheaded by *Today* (今天, 1978–1980), which first published what quickly became known as Obscure or Misty poetry, by authors including Bei Dao, Shu Ting, Gu Cheng, Yang Lian and Duoduo. *Today* was closed down by the police within two years. Short-lived as the journal was, it had a huge impact among urban intellectuals.

Han Dong (韩东) was doubtless inspired by *Today*, and his very early work—now lost to his readers, with the exception of hardcore literary historians—still reflected a tragic-heroic poetics associated with Obscure Poetry, but he soon radically changed his style. "Mountain People" (1982, page 32 in the present volume) was a harbinger of trends that would take center stage from the mid-1980s onward, when Han became founding editor of *Them* (他们, 1984–1995), one of the most renowned and enduring of the underground journals. If the poem alludes to the fable of the Foolish Old Man Moving the Mountain and its Maoist redux, it takes an ironic turn when its protagonist grows tired, in contradistinction to the Old Man's unflinching determination and perseverance; and *within* the avant-garde, it deviates sharply from the grandiloquence and the daring metaphors of Obscure Poetry that were *en vogue* at the time.

[*] Reworked from *Chinese Poetry in Times of Mind, Mayhem and Money* (Leiden / Boston: Brill, 2008), Chapter Two. An earlier version appeared in the *Tamkang Review* Vol. 36 No. 4 (2006).

"Mountain People" presaged two of Han's best-known poems, "Of the Wild Goose Pagoda" (1982, page 30) and "So You've Seen the Sea" (1983, page 34). Written in the same deceptively simple style, they display skepticism, irony and an effective type of reticence, things that had been in exceptionally short supply in orthodox poetry and in the earliest stages of the avant-garde. Specifically, "Of the Wild Goose Pagoda" and "So You've Seen the Sea" write back to famous poems by Yang Lian and Shu Ting, deconstructing Yang's conventional, bombastic literary presentation of the Pagoda as a proud landmark of Chinese civilization (and the average Chinese tourist's supposed consciousness of same), and Shu Ting's exalted hymns to the ocean.

As such, the early Han Dong rejected the high-sounding ideals of both literary orthodoxy and the early avant-garde, and offered a forceful commentary on what was then the most influential modern poetry in China, after literature's emancipation from total political control. His dictum that "poetry goes no farther than language" brings to mind Mallarmé's remark that poetry is made of words not ideas (even if this is a gross simplification of Mallarmé's poetics). Han's words breathe a similar desire to demystify poetry and poethood, or minimally to emphasize the primacy of language as poetry's medium, rather than representing poetry as an extension or remediation of anything else: say, of Truth or Beauty, or of the poet as prophet, seer, or otherwise exceptional and glamorous human being.

As regards thematics, scholarship has focused on Han's low-key deconstruction of conventional topoi and his predilection for the quotidian, for the trivia of everyday life. It has paid insufficient attention to Han's regular deployment of shock effects caused by the interruption of monotony or smoothness, especially powerful when an abrupt turn in the poem's semantics occurs without a change in its prosody or other formal features. In "Of the Wild Goose Pagoda," this happens in the offhand mention of individuals jumping to their deaths, in a disturbing contrast with gregarious tourists eager to share in the glory of a public landmark. In "So You've Seen the Sea," nearly the entire poem is reserved for building up a hypnotic drone through repetition and near-repetition. Then, the speaker shatters the monotony by picturing *you* as drowning and the sea *you* likes to romanticize as a killer, without a ripple in the poem's form. Then, too, we realize that the observation "But you're not / A sailor," halfway through the poem, was a warning. By association with the sea as a popular image across literary traditions, Han Dong implies an opposition of the poet, as one who speaks of the sea but has no right, versus the sailor, as one who has the right but doesn't speak.

In addition, Han Dong's presentation of his themes is often enhanced by a willed superficiality on the part of the speaker. This is not so much a sign of the postmodern as a mechanism of defamiliarization that blocks out conventional dynamics of reason, emotion, and association. The flat, objectivist observations made in "Of the Wild Goose Pagoda" don't lead to soul-searching or value judgment, and subvert seemingly self-evident assumptions: that landmarks like the Pagoda enable individuals to experience their cultural heritage, that poetry is a suitable vehicle for expressing that experience, or—with reference to the classical Chinese tradition—that ascending a high point to take in the view is a suitable theme for a poem. The speaker merely observes that all sorts of people come to the Pagoda, climb up, look around and perhaps enjoy the illusion of being heroes, and then come down again, with the suicides as a terrifying aside whose exploration is left to the reader. The repression of common knowledge and conventional discourse has a profoundly defamiliarizing effect, summed up in the question the poem asks in the beginning and again at the end: "What do we really know," its resignation to our ignorance visible in the absence of a question mark.

Critics have habitually called Han Dong's language usage colloquial, and colloquial language has been among the claims to fame of many Chinese poets since *Them* first appeared, and continues to be high on the critical agenda. Scholars and poets alike have pointed out that this so-called colloquial language is not the same as that spoken in ordinary human traffic, but the label is reasonable enough, certainly in its immediate literary-historical context. However, in this respect the power of Han Dong's poetry lies not just in the rejection of formal or high registers. Positively defined, his usage comes across as measured, focused and controlled. This lends his poetry a feeling of quiet confidence, palpable concentration, and insistence. His word choice tallies well with the form of his poetry: free verse, with short lines.

Perhaps inevitably, the canonization of a small number of Han Dong's early poems as primarily "colloquial" trendsetters has led to the neglect of other features of his work. Clichés about his work that simplify what are in fact complex literary texts have no way of capturing the full breadth of his oeuvre. "Someone in a Riot of Stones" (1988, page 4), for instance, isn't about the trivia of everyday life at all. Instead, in one possible reading, it allows the imagination to transform a human being into a reptile, then athlete, then stone, then human being again, and then cold-blooded, crawling animal again. The poem displays no objectivism of any kind, and is syntactically ambiguous and enigmatic, not to say inaccessible: What enclosure? Is the protagonist inside or outside the brickwork? Who are *we*? What happens next? The text is intriguing, and it definitely invites the classification of images as metaphors, different from Han's professed what-you-see-is-what-you-get poetics. Most importantly, the poetic voice expresses tension, complete engagement, and anything but irony.

Just like "Someone in a Riot of Stones," "There Is a Darkness" (1988, page 6) contains enigmatic, surrealist scenes and literary techniques not normally associated with the demystification that is known as a trademark of Han Dong's poetry. With twelve occurrences in fourteen lines, *darkness* acquires incantatory qualities. The poem's language is not difficult, but not colloquial either: "Darkness that weakens lights scattered evenly / Across a thousand miles to their lowest glow." An important scene in this poem is that of four people walking off in four different directions. Their separation and the increasing distance between them take the form of the darkness that gives the poem its name. Then, separation and distance are projected on the trees. There is darkness between them: not because they stand close together, but of a mutually unwelcoming kind. The observation that this darkness forbids strangers to enter projects it back from the trees on the four human beings, and shows their inability to establish and maintain company and contact, a notion that recurs throughout Han's oeuvre.

"A and B" (1991, page 36) is something of a *pièce de résistance* in Han Dong's oeuvre. The protagonists' designation as A and B (甲乙 in Chinese, the first two of the ten Heavenly Stems, employed as serial numbers for unspecified enumeration) depersonalizes them more effectively than would have been the case had Han Dong used pronouns. In an instance of the aforesaid willed superficiality, the speaker isn't satisfied by noting that A spends a short while looking out the window before bending over to tie his shoes, but describes his every movement in minute detail. For a different plot—say, the operation of hi-tech machinery in preparation for robbing a bank—this type of description could produce tension that builds up to a climax. Here, however, it is as if behavior such as A's, or indeed the very existence of his species, is perceived for the first time and fails to activate any ready framework for the construction of meaning. This explains the speaker's inability to be selective, and the obsessive recording of detail. All this happens in a language not unlike that of scientific observation: the geometry of A's attempts to see more of the tree, quantification of the shifts in his physical position, the use of words like *disparity*. The speaker moves from depersonalization to dehumanization, by stating what is the obvious in everyday human experience.

In the transition in which A goes from looking out the window to closing his eyes and finishing the tying of his shoes, it is yet again the mechanism of defamiliarization that produces a line of reasoning that is not illogical in itself—as reasoning without a reasoner, if there is such a thing—but that we know to be untrue, and somehow find funny to imagine. We are not sure why A closes and opens and closes his eyes again. Is he testing his vision? But then we realize that to the speaker, this makes perfect sense. A is done looking out the window, and doesn't need to look at his feet while tying his shoes. Hence, he stops looking by "switching off" his eyes, just like one stops chewing once the food is swallowed and gone from the mouth.

"A and B" shows Han Dong at his most sophisticated in manipulating the quotidian as poetic material. If we decide to interpret what is offered to us at face value, an important part of the message is that entire worlds lie behind the tiniest of details, in poetry and possibly elsewhere in life. Another key component of the interpretation, in line with the poems reviewed above, is a cynical view of human togetherness and interaction. In the opening lines, A and B are sitting with their backs to one another. B disappears from view until the closing scene. There, the speaker observes that A has neglected B, and that A and B see different things, and don't see one another. A sees the world outside the window; B sees household chores. This is an ironic mobilization of clichéd, reactionary visions of heterosexual marriage.

A's sperm *leaving* B's body when she gets up—that is, distancing itself from her—confirms their fundamental separation. This holds in the defamiliarized outsider's view that represses common knowledge, in this case of the physical details of sexual intercourse and mechanisms of reproduction. Neither the physical togetherness of sex nor a possible pregnancy would do anything to change this view, in which human contact is little more than a chance meeting of monads incapable of real interaction. Conversely, any (naive) association of sex with things like romantic love would make the speaker's portrayal of A and B as ignoring one another after having had sex nothing short of painful, and the ending to the poem (naively) scandalous and shocking.

*

Several things combine to make Han Dong the remarkable poet he is: quotidian themes, willed superficiality, colloquial language, and his individuality and sophistication in handling these things. Or, conversely: the *deconstruction* of heroic themes, the *repression* of conventional interpretation, the *rejection* of "literary" language, and *defamiliarization* as a fundamental textual attitude.

The first list of features would make Han Dong's poetry one that believes in authenticity, and in personal experience as the measure of all things, sometimes to the point of absurdity. The second makes it a poetry that *disbelieves* in affectation, and in anything that lies outside personal experience. Both perspectives are rewarding. But there is one important theme that is impossible to fit into the first list and easy to add to the second, and that makes Han Dong a disbeliever after all. That is this poetry's skepticism regarding human contact and communication, including communication through poetry. As such, it helps perpetuate a paradox that is very much part of the singularity of the genre.

A Phone Call from Dalian

Nicky Harman

I was struck when reading Maghiel's excellent essay on Han Dong that while we share an admiration for Han Dong's poetry, we take very different things from his work. What follows are my personal impressions, as a reader and as a translator, of the work of one of my favorite poets.

As Maghiel explains, Han Dong in the 1980s was known for being in-your-face iconoclastic, a poet who robustly avoided high-flown poetic sentiment and metaphor, and looked into himself and those around him for inspiration. While that is still true of his work, he has developed a varied poetic voice over the last three decades, and this collection is representative of that variety.

In much of his love poetry, there is an emotional directness and a simplicity which is beguiling. In "The Days of Our Lives," love becomes a bumpy train ride: "Life rocks and shakes us/Hold me tighter!" Poems such as "Under the Streetlights of Shenzhen," on the other hand, contain complex, multi-layered images of water, color and light: "infernal river . . . black waves", bright lights "like piled-up glass." Then there are the raunchy ones, "The Worker's Hand," for instance, with its "A woman should fall in love with that hand/Should receive its caresses/A man should have a hand like this/Strong, grimy, like a fleshy sucker pad" as well as its sly humor.

Bust-ups and bereavement are themes of some of the tenderest poems in this collection. "News" is bittersweet, "The last time we made love/No one knew it was the last time." So is "So Dispassionate": "Someone's distance/Another's death/Two ways of leaving us."

There is an implicit warmth towards women which is by turns ironic and sympathetic. (This is not a characteristic universally shared by contemporary male writers in China.) So we read about his elderly neighbors in "Summertime Window": "A cluster of old women/Exercise in the courtyard/Bending and stretching/Waving their arms/All moving to a different beat." And the widowed countrywoman in "Visiting Shandong," whose dignity is contrasted with the narrator's foolish grin. Then there is the girl who may or may not sell her body as well as noodles, in "Waitress" (the word waitress in Chinese can also mean prostitute) and the prostitute in "Under the Streetlights." This sympathy runs all through his work, for example in the apparently throwaway line in "Night Flight," "Those who became our faithful wives / Are still subjected to our arrogant gaze" and in the outcome of "A and B" when B, who sees only the unwashed dishes, is finally revealed to be a woman.

Certain poems have a strong sense of stillness which demands an equal stillness in the reader. Han Dong paints a picture (often precisely descriptive) and then presents us with a freeze-frame: the chopping board and broken cup in "A Loud Noise," the settling oil in "A Calm." One of our translators, Yu Yan Chen, calls this quality "very Zen" but, although there are Buddhist references, for example to the "world of nothingness" in "Making a Note," Han Dong's poetry is not explicitly Buddhist.

Then there are the frankly surreal poems, which depart from his usual apparent simplicity of image and language, and are full of shifting perspectives. In "Absurd Winter Scene," for instance, the perspective shifts between the scene itself and its representation on paper, or between the "tree branch drawn in charcoal" and its burning "once again into a stick of charcoal."

When Han Dong breaks taboos, the result can be startlingly intimate. In "Pain," he graphically describes a young woman dying: "Pain gives this once sweet compliant girl / The stubborn rigidity of a corpse." The tone here is not ironic and detached, as in "Of the Wild Goose Pagoda," but one of deeply felt emotion. He has written a poem on menstruation (not included) and one on defecation—"In White-tiled Brightness"—which describes the comings and goings in a monastery toilet with tongue-in-cheek gravity. (Not perhaps obviously offensive, but my translation was turned down by the publication which originally commissioned it on the grounds that it was inappropriate to associate crapping and childbirth!)

Han Dong lived in the Chinese countryside as a boy. It was the time of the Cultural Revolution (the subject of his first novel in translation, *Banished!*) and he and his parents were re-settled in a poor, remote village. The experience, far from being wholly negative, gave him a lasting nostalgia for the countryside and its people, and the rhythms of farming life. We see this in two poems in this collection: "The Softer Part" and "Wood Work." In the former he says that country life brings out the gentler side of his character, and likens his own pain and frustration to the anguish that the farmer suffers over the death of his/her crops. In the latter, he writes an unadorned poem, almost hypnotic in its repetitions, about the poverty of the life of woodworkers he knew in his youth. Something is lost in the translation of this short poem: the characters "木工" can equally mean "wood work," the activity, and "wood workers," the people. When I asked Han Dong which he thought I should choose, he said whichever I liked, which raises interesting questions about the role of the translator in his poetry.

Most of Han Dong's poems are lyrical and stand alone. We have included here, however, one sequence with a narrative thread (starting from "Night Flight" in this collection). In 1994, Han Dong paid his first visit to the burgeoning and glitzy New Economic Zone of Shenzhen, at that time dramatically different from the rest of China. Here he shows no interest in "learning by example" from the hard-working Shenzhen entrepreneurs but instead an avid interest in living it up with friends and a "slide into debauchery" involving visits to prostitutes. While these four poems have appeared in magazines separately, they also form an entertaining sequence.

We have said that Han Dong eschews grand themes, especially of the patriotic and nationalistic kind. In an apparent exception to this, in "Visiting Shandong," he describes a trip to the Northeast, an area which was fought over by the Russians, then the Japanese and the Chinese, and suffered a long period of Japanese occupation in the first half of the twentieth century.

* University of Hawai'i Press, 2008.

However, although moved by the area's historical associations, he typically focuses on the people who live there. He describes meeting a woman who has lost her husband in a road accident, and remains alone in a village stripped of its inhabitants by China's pell-mell economic development; and, typically, he invests her with a dignity which is forcibly contrasted with the foolish smiles he and his friends give her.

In Chinese literary circles, Han Dong is an opinionated defender of what he believes in, arguing in essays, blogs and published exchanges with other writers, against both Party-sponsored literary prizes and other blandishments, and the hectic commercialization of the literary world. Little of this bellicosity finds a place in his poems; mostly, he confines himself to sly mockery, for instance of ultra-patriotism in "Of the Wild Goose Pagoda." However, there is the occasional line here and there in this collection which sounds a censorious note. In "It's Foggy," he criticizes "knee-jerk reactions" over "prescient actions" (the Chinese, "全知全能," is a rather high-flown four-character phrase meaning "omniscient and omnipotent"). And at the end of "Elevator Door Etc.," "The gate of intelligence is tightly shut" . . . and we are quite sure he is not referring to himself.

Han Dong is still best-known in the West for his early, iconic poems such as "Of the Wild Goose Pagoda." So it is gratifying to be able to redress the balance now: in this short collection, we have brought together for readers some outstanding poems which display the range of Han Dong's work over three decades. You will find them, by turns, disconcerting, meditative, angry, passionate, sad, sarcastic, self-mocking and even a little silly. I hope you will enjoy them as much as I do.

★

My sincere thanks go, firstly, to Han Dong, for having faith in our translations; also to Xiaomu Cheng and Brian Holton for their encouragement and practical help (and to many other friends and colleagues, please consider yourselves thanked even if there is no space to name you); and, of course, to my husband Brin for all his love and support.

Thank you to the editors who published earlier versions of these poems in the following journals and anthologies:

"Crossing the Lingdingyang, the Lonely Sea" and "Waitress" appeared in *Push Open the Window: Contemporary Poetry from China,* Copper Canyon Press, 2011.

"It's Foggy" appeared in *Chutzpah* No. 4, 2011.

"So You've Seen the Sea," "A and B," "Of the Wild Goose Pagoda," "Mountain People," "There Is a Darkness," and "Someone in a Riot of Stones" appeared in *Chinese Poetry in Times of Mind, Mayhem and Money,* Brill, 2011.

"Let Me Describe the Rainstorm," "Green Tree, Red Fruit," "Growing Up Is a Mistake," and "The Days of Our Lives" appeared in *Renditions* No. 74, 2010.

"A Phone Call from Dalian" and "Some People Don't Like to Talk" appeared in *Modern Poetry in Translation, Polyphony,* Series 3 No. 14, 2010.

"In White-tiled Brightness" appeared in *Point Barre, Revue de Poésie,* 2009.

"The Softer Part," "Under the Streetlights of Shenzhen" and "Return" appeared in *Eight Contemporary Chinese Poets,* Wild Peony, 2006.

"Under the Streetlights of Shenzhen," "Return" and "Night Flight" appeared in *Renditions* No. 57, 2002.

A PHONE CALL FROM DALIAN

来自大连的电话

绿树、红果

我不在的时候绿树在那里
然后我走过了它
然后绿树的前面还有绿树
树杈中间有太阳

我直视太阳，此刻
它就像红果
因此整个园子都成了果园

一些足音纷至沓来
嗡嗡的人声议论着生活
人影如虫蠓盘旋、聚集
金星如一滴大大的清凉的眼泪

我仍然在那里
红果已经消失
绿树失色

Green Tree, Red Fruit

The green tree was there before I was
Then I walked past it
Then ahead of the tree, there were more green trees
Between the forked branches was the sun

I looked right at the sun. Just then
It was like a red fruit
And so the whole garden became an orchard

A flurry of footsteps came
A buzzing of voices debated life
People's shadows circled, gathered like gnats
The evening star, a great cool teardrop

I am still there
The red fruit gone
The green trees dulled

(2008)

一堆乱石中的一个人

一堆乱石中的一个人。一个
这样的人，这样的一堆乱石

爬行者，紧贴地面的人
缓慢移动甚至不动的蜥蜴

乱石间时而跳跃的运动员，或是
石块上面降落的石块

不是一面围墙下的那个人
整齐而规则的砖缝前面的那个人

当我们注视时停止在那里
把一块石头的温度传递给另一块石头

它的形状是六块相互重叠的石头
现在，渴求雨水似地爬到了
画面的上方

Someone in a Riot of Stones

Someone in a riot of stones. Someone
Like that, a riot of stones like that

Crawler, one hugging the ground
Slowly moving, even unmoving lizard

Athlete leaping amid riotous stones, or
Stone falling down on stones

It's not the one at the foot of an enclosure
The one before the neat and orderly brickwork

Stops right there when we stare
Transfers one stone's warmth to another

Its shape is six stones overlapping
Now, as if craving rainwater, crawls
Onto the picture

(1988)

一种黑暗

我注意到林子里的黑暗
有差别的黑暗
广场一样的黑暗在树林中
四个人向四个方向走去造成的黑暗
在树木中间但不是树木内部的黑暗
向上升起扩展到整个天空的黑暗
不是地下的岩石不分彼此的黑暗
使千里之外的灯光分散平均
减弱到最低限度的黑暗
经过一万棵树的转折没有消失的黑暗
有一种黑暗在任何时间中禁止陌生人入内
如果你伸出一只手揽动它就是
巨大的玻璃杯中的黑暗
我注意到林子里的黑暗虽然我不在林中

There Is a Darkness

I notice the darkness of the forest
Darkness with a difference
Darkness like a square, in the forest
Darkness made by four people walking off in four directions
Darkness between the trees but not inside the trees
Darkness rising spreading through the sky
Darkness not of underground rocks that share everything
Darkness that weakens lights scattered evenly
Across a thousand miles to their lowest glow
Darkness gone through turns of endless trees, not vanished
There is a darkness that forbids strangers to enter at any time
If you reach out a hand to stir it that is
Darkness in a giant glass
I notice the darkness of the forest though I am not in the forest

(1988)

我听见杯子

这时，我听见杯子
一连串美妙的声音
单调而独立
最清醒的时刻
强大或微弱
城市，在它光明的核心
需要这样一些光芒
安放在桌上
需要一些投影
医好他们的创伤
水的波动，烟的飘散
他们习惯于夜晚的姿势
清新可爱，依然
是他们的本钱
依然有百分之一的希望
使他们度过纯洁的一生
真正的黑暗在远方吼叫
可杯子依然响起
清脆，激越
被握在手中

I Hear Cups

At this moment, I hear cups
A series of exquisite sounds
Monotonous, detached
At their clearest
Formidable or faint
The city, at its brilliant core
Needs some of this luster
Placed on a table
Some shadows are needed
To heal their wounds
The undulation of water, the dispersal of smoke
They're used to the night's postures
Purity and charm
Are still their estate
They still have a one percent hope
To lead a pure life
In the distance true darkness howls
But the cup still chimes
Clearly, intensely
Held in a hand

(1987)

一声巨响

一声巨响
我走出去查看
什么也没有看见

一小时后
我发现砧板
落在灶台上
砸碎了一只杯子

砧板丝纹不动
杯子的碎片也是
静静的

当初砧板挂在墙上
杯子在它的下面
也是静静的

A Loud Noise

A loud noise
I went out to check
Nothing

An hour later
I discovered the chopping board
Fallen on the cook top
A broken cup

The chopping board lay still
Fragments of the cup were also
Quite quiet

The chopping board used to hang on the wall
The cup beneath it
Both quite quiet

(2001)

山东行

驱车行驶在山东的土地上
意识到，这是老区，这是老区
看见了白杨树，啊，永远的白杨树
灰蒙蒙的远山，仿佛有硝烟漂浮其间
石头垒砌的院墙像堡垒一样结实
悬挂的玉米棒子何时迸裂——像手雷
将和平的种子撒向这贫瘠的山乡
在这里，战争似乎已经获得永生
就像一块土地的季节性休耕
战时的儿女不改沧桑坚毅的面容

仿佛在一部老电影里旅行，或者
正在撰写新的传奇
大娘的三个儿子都在城里上班
她和老伴坚守在走空了的村子里
去年老伴也被一辆农用汽车轧死了
对方无钱赔偿，进了班房
大娘的脸上没有悲戚，颜色
就像她卖的栗子一样深
我们冲大娘咧嘴憨笑，直到牙龈毕露
犹如这漫山遍野绽开的红石榴

Visiting Shandong

Driving across the land of Shandong
It dawns on me — this is the Old Liberated Area, the Old Liberated Area!*
I see the white poplars, oh, the eternal white poplars
Far away, the hazy mountains seem wreathed in gun smoke
The courtyards built of stones sturdy as fortresses
When will those hanging cobs of corn burst — like hand grenades
Spraying seeds of peace at this barren countryside
Here the war seems to have gained eternal life
Like a land left seasonally fallow
The children of war never shed their look of weathered perseverance

We could be travelling through an old film
Or composing a new legend
The old lady's three sons all work in the city
She and her husband stayed to guard the emptied village
Last year her husband was hit by a farm truck and killed
The driver had no money to pay her and went to jail
Yet her face bears no trace of sadness, is as deeply coloured
As the chestnuts she sells
We grin foolishly at her, showing all of our gums
Red as pomegranate blossoms bursting over fields and hillsides

(2009)

---

* The Old Liberated Areas are sections of China controlled by the Communists pre-1949.

来自大连的电话

一个来自大连的电话，她也不是
我昔日的情人。没有目的。电话
仅在叙述自己的号码。一个女人
让我回忆起三年前流行的一种容貌

刚刚结婚，在飘满油漆味儿的新房
正适应和那些庄严的家具在一起
（包括一部亲自选购的电话）
也许只是出于好奇（象年轻的母猫）
她在摆弄丈夫财产的同时，偶尔
拨通了给我的电话？

大连古老的海浪是否在她的窗前？
是否有一块当年的礁石仍在坚持
感人的形象？多年以后——不会太久
如果仍有那来自中年的电话，她一定
学会了生活。三十年后
只有波涛，在我的右耳
我甚至听不见她粗重的母兽的呼吸

A Phone Call from Dalian

A phone call from Dalian. It wasn't even
A former lover. It was pointless. The call
Simply gave her phone number. A woman
Made me think back to a type of face popular three years ago.

She was just married, in a new house smelling of fresh paint
Which went perfectly with the stately furniture
(Including the phone she'd personally picked)
Was it perhaps just from curiosity (like a young cat)
That, as she fiddled with her husband's possessions, she happened
To dial my number?

Were Dalian's ancient waves lapping outside her window?
Was there that rock, still insisting on
Its stirring image? If, many years later — but not too long
She were to call again, from middle age, she would certainly
Have learned about life. Thirty years later
There would just be waves, in my right ear
I would not even hear her harsh, she-animal breathing.

(2008)

一种平静

激烈变得平静了
就是激烈也无法持久
动荡之后，秩序来临
表面的张力维持住这些油
油，而不是水
集中于这只端平的碗中
不再点燃像血
不再四处奔流

A Calm

Intensity calms down
Even intensity cannot last
After the chaos, order arrives
Surface elasticity sustains these oils
Oil, not water
Collecting in this level bowl
No longer burns like blood
No longer overflowing everywhere

(2003)

圆玉

熄灯以后，黑暗降临
稳定之后，有一点光亮
隐约的，让我惊奇
这绿光我从未见过
然后，我的手摸到了一块圆玉
连着它的线绳绕着我的手指
无法追忆为谁所赠
后来想起来了
这收敛的光仍然陌生
不照亮附近的任何物体
幽暗有如盲人眼中的光明

Round Jade

When the light goes out, darkness descends
When it settles, a gleam of light appears
Flickering, what could it be? I wonder
I've never seen this greenish glow before
Then my hand touches a piece of round jade
Connected to a string that winds around my fingers
Can't recall who gave it to me
(Though later I remember)
This restrained glow still seems strange:
It illuminates nothing else around it
Dim as brightness to the blind

(2003)

雨

什么事都没有的时候
下雨是一件大事
一件事正在发生的时候
雨成为背景
有人记住了，有人忘记了
很多年后，一切已成为过去
雨又来到眼前
淅淅沥沥地下着
没有什么事发生

Rain

Rain is a major event
When nothing else happens
It recedes into the background
While an event unfolds
Some remember it, some forget
Years later, when all is past
Rain reappears before our eyes
Falling as fine drizzle
Nothing much is happening

(2002)

格里高里圣歌

唱歌的人在户外
在高寒地区
仰着脖子
把歌声送上去
就像松树
把叶子送上去
唱着唱着
就变成了坚硬的松木
一排排的

Gregorian Chant

The singer sings outdoors
In a cold, high place
Like a pine tree that offers up
Its leaves
He sends the songs upwards
Head thrown back
Chanting and chanting
Into rows and rows
Of sturdy pine trees

(2002)

电梯门及其它

电梯的门打开，又关上了
一些人从里面出来，另一些人
又进去
就像门后有一所很大的房子
人们在那儿安家，就像
有一个大厅或者大会议室
需要用麦克风讲话

一些人的嘴张开，又闭上了
在反复的开合之间，一些词语
从里面出来，一些冷风
窜了进去
就像他们来自一个大地方，来自世界
就像我所在的世界不是我的
仅仅是他们的

在电梯门的背后
只有深井，一只金属箱子或者盒子
那些词语的背后有着同样的狭窄和局促
聪明之门已经关上了

Elevator Door Etc.

The elevator door opens, then shuts again
Some people step out, others
Step in
As though a huge house awaits them
People settle down there, as if
There's a hall or an enormous conference room
And to speak, one needs a microphone

Some mouths open, then shut again
Open and close constantly as words
Step out, and cold winds
Rush in
As though coming from an enormous place, from the world
As if the world I'm in does not belong to me
But only to them

Beyond the elevator door
There's only a deep shaft, a metal case or box
What's beyond those words is just as cramped and narrow
The gate of intelligence is tightly shut

(2009)

工人的手

他悬挂在高楼上
抓着墙的手纹丝不动
我觉得是女人就应该爱上这只手
就应该接受它的抚摩
是男人就应该有这样的手
结实、肮脏，像吸盘肉垫
是女人就应该做那面墙
降低一些吧
最好躺下
是男人就应该死死地抓住那女人
浑身大汗淋漓，但手不出汗
心不跳，腿也不抖
如果是个恋物癖就这样恋吧
工人的手也是最棒的工具

The Worker's Hand

He hangs suspended from the building
The hand that grips the wall is motionless
A woman should fall in love with that hand
Should receive its caresses
A man should have a hand like this
Strong, grimy, like a fleshy sucker pad
A woman should be that wall
Drop down a bit, or better still,
Lie down
A man should hold that woman in a vice-like grip
His body soaked in sweat (but not his hand
No leaping heart or quivering legs)
If this is fetishism, then lets love this way
The worker's hand is a marvellous tool

(2010)

卖鸡的

他拥有迅速杀鸡的技艺，因此
成了一个卖鸡的，这样
他就不需要杀人，即使在心里
他的生活平静温馨，从不打老婆
脱去老婆的衣服就像给鸡褪毛
相似的技艺总有相通之处
残暴与温柔也总是此消彼长
当他脱鸡毛、他老婆慢腾腾地收钱的时候
我总觉得这里面有某种罪恶的甜蜜

The Chicken Seller

He's got the knack for killing chickens quick, so
He became a chicken-seller, that way
He doesn't need to kill people. Even though he acts
Calm and gentle, and never beats his wife
Taking off his wife's clothes is like plucking a chicken
Similar skills always overlap, just as
Cruelty and kindness are two sides of the same coin
He plucks, and she leisurely takes the money
And I feel that therein lies a kind of evil sweetness

(2009)

有关大雁塔

我们又能知道些什么
有很多人从远方赶来
为了爬上去
做一次英雄
也有的还来做第二次
或者更多
那些不得意的人们
那些发福的人们
统统爬上去
做一做英雄
然后下来
走进这条大街
转眼不见了
也有有种的往下跳
在台阶上开一朵红花
那就真的成了英雄
当代英雄

有关大雁塔
我们又能知道什么
我们爬上去
看看四周的风景
然后再下来

Of the Wild Goose Pagoda

Of the Wild Goose Pagoda
What do we really know
Many people come rushing from afar
To climb up
And be a hero
Some come a second time
Or even more than that
People not pleased with themselves
People grown stout
They all climb up
To be that hero
And then they come down
Walk into the road below
And disappear in the blink of an eye
The real gutsy ones jump down
Red flowers blooming on the steps
Now there's a real hero
A hero of our time

Of the Wild Goose Pagoda
What do we really know
We climb up
Look at the view around us
And then come down again

(1982)

山民

小时侯，他问父亲
"山的那边是什么"
父亲说"是山"
"那边的那边呢"
"山，还是山"
他不作声了，看着远处
山第一次使他这样疲倦

他想，这辈子是走不出这里的群山了
海是有的，但十分遥远
他只能活几十年
所以没有等他走到那里
就已死在半路上了
死在山中

他觉得应该带着老婆一起上路
老婆会给他生个儿子
到他死的时候
儿子就长大了
儿子也会有老婆
儿子也会有儿子
儿子的儿子也还会有儿子
他不再想了
儿子也使他很疲惫

他只是遗憾
他的祖先没有像他一样想过
不然，见到大海的该是他了

Mountain People

As a child, he asked his father
"What's beyond the mountains"
His father said "mountains"
"And beyond beyond"
"Mountains, more mountains"
He made no sound, looking in the distance
For the first time, the mountains made him tired

He thought he couldn't get out of the mountains in this life
The sea was there, but far away
And he could only live a couple dozen years
So before he'd get there
He'd die halfway
Die in the mountains

He felt he should set out together with his old lady
His old lady would give him a son
And by the time he died
His son would have grown up
And his son would have an old lady too
And his son would have a son too
And his son's son would have a son too
He stopped thinking
His son made him tired too

He only regretted
His ancestors hadn't thought that way
Or the one to see the sea would have been him

(1982)

你见过大海

你见过大海
你想象过
大海
你想象过大海
然后见到它
就是这样
你见过了大海
并想象过它
可你不是
一个水手
就是这样
你想象过大海
你见过大海
也许你还喜欢大海
最多是这样
你见过大海
你也想象过大海
你不情愿
让海水给淹死
就是这样
人人都这样

So You've Seen the Sea

So you've seen the sea
You've imagined
The sea
You've imagined the sea
And then seen it
Just like this
So now you've really seen the sea
And imagined it as well
But you're not
A sailor
Just like this
So you've imagined the sea
You've seen the sea
Perhaps you even like the sea
Just like this, and nothing more
So you've seen the sea
And you've imagined the sea
You're not willing
To be drowned by the sea
Just like this
Just like everybody else

(1983)

甲乙

甲乙二人分别从床的两边下床
甲在系鞋带。背对着他的乙也在系鞋带
甲的前面是一扇窗户，因此他看见了街景
和一根横过来的树枝。树身被墙挡住了
因此他只好从刚要被挡住的地方往回看
树枝，越来越细，直到末梢
离另一边的墙，还有好大一截
空着，什么也没有，没有树枝、街景
也许仅仅是天空。甲再（第二次）往回看
头向左移了五厘米，或向前
也移了五厘米，或向左的同时也向前
不止五厘米，总之是为了看得更多
更多的树枝，更少的空白。左眼比右眼
看得更多。它们之间的距离是三厘米
但多看见的树枝都不止三厘米
他（甲）以这样的差距再看街景
闭上左眼，然后闭上右眼睁开左眼
然后再闭上左眼。到目前为止两只眼睛
都已闭上。甲什么也不看。甲系鞋带的时候
不用看，不用看自己的脚，先左后右
两只都已系好了。四岁时就已学会
五岁受到表扬，六岁已很熟练
这是甲七岁以后的某一天，三十岁的某一天或
六十岁的某一天，他仍能弯腰系自己的鞋带
只是把乙忽略得太久了。这是我们
（首先是作者）与甲一起犯下的错误
她（乙）从另一边下床，面对一只碗柜

A and B

Two people A and B sit up on opposite sides of the bed
A is tying his shoes. So is B, back turned to A
In front of A there's a window, so that he looks out on the street
And a horizontal tree branch. The tree trunk is obstructed by the wall
So that, from this obstruction, he must look back
Along the tree branch, ever thinner, all the way to the end
After which, before the next stretch of wall, there's still a large
Empty space, nothing there, neither tree branch nor street
Maybe only empty sky. A (a second time) looks back again
Head moving five centimeters leftward, or five centimeters
Forward too, or even more than five centimeters leftward and forward
At the same time, anyway, with the aim of looking at more
And more tree branch, and less emptiness. The left eye can look at more
Than the right. The distance between them is three centimeters
But the extra bit of tree branch looked at is more than three centimeters
Using this disparity, he (A) looks once again at the street
Closes his left eye, then closes his right and opens his left
Then closes his left again. At this point both eyes
Are closed. A looks at nothing. When A ties his shoes
There's no need to look, no need to look at his feet, first left then right
Now both are tied. At four he knew how
At five he was commended, at six he was skilled
This is a day in A's life after seven, a day when he's thirty-something or
A day when he's sixty-something, and can still bend over to tie his shoes
It's just that he's neglected B for too long. This is our
(First of all the author's) and A's joint mistake
She (B) sits up on the bed's opposite side, facing a cupboard

隔着玻璃或纱窗看见了甲所没有看见的餐具
为叙述的完整起见还必须指出
当乙系好鞋带起立，流下了本属于甲的精液

Looks through the glass or the screen and sees dishes that A doesn't see
To bring this narration to a close, let it be noted that
When B has tied her shoes and stands, sperm trickles down that was once A's

(1991)

你的手

你的手搭在我的身上
安心睡去
我因此而无法入睡
轻微的重量
逐渐变成铅
夜晚又很长
你的姿态毫不改变
这只手应该象征着爱情
也许还另有深意
我不敢推动它
或惊醒你
等到我习惯并且喜欢
你在梦中又突然把手抽回
并对一切无从知晓

Your Hand

Your hand placed on my body
You go to sleep at peace
And because of this I cannot sleep
Its slight weight
Gradually grows into lead
The night is very long
Your position does not shift
This hand ought to signify love
Possibly it has yet another deep meaning
I dare not push it away
Or startle you awake
When I grow used to it and like it too
In dreams suddenly you take back the hand
And are oblivious to all this

(1986)

火车

火车从很远的地方经过
你曾是那个坐在车厢里的孩子
远离我所在的城市，或者回来
在黑夜阻隔的途中

我也曾靠在床头
等待着你的归来
你也曾向你的父母告假
那假期多长多甜蜜！

有时我多么想驶近你
只因受到车轮滚动的激励
一阵风自远方吹来在远方平息
猛烈的汽笛终于变成了柔和的炊烟
飘向我

当火车从远方经过
因为遥远所以蜿蜒
因为黑夜所以动听
因为你，使我看见了良辰美景

The Train

The train came from far away
You were the girl sitting in the carriage
Going far from the city where I was, or coming back
Separated by the dark night

I sat up in bed
Waiting for your return
You asked your parents if you could take the time
It was a long time, and so sweet!

Galvanised by the rolling of the train wheels,
I sometimes longed to speed to you
The wind gusted from far away and, far away, subsided
The fierce whistle turned to gentle smoke
Wafting towards me

When the train came from far away
Because of the distance, it meandered
Because of the night, it sounded sweet
Because of you, I saw the scenery was lovely

(1995)

写这场雨

写这场雨
它是极其普通的
并且已经停息
昨夜雨打在宽阔的叶子上
使得整棵梧桐都颤动起来

我经历了无数个这样的夜晚
有时候还在路上
老远
看见窗户上的灯光
向着黑暗中的风雨打开
可走到窗下
还要好长的时间

昨夜我坐在房子里
我的窗户也已关闭
我的灯光熄灭了
雨打在叶子上
又清脆的落到地上

这是一场春雨
花儿不会因此凋零
只有喜悦的啜泣声
在周围的世界里此起彼伏的

看来这样的雨还要再下几场
才能吐尽各人心中的悲欢
而真正的幸福降临
是一道阳光
照在林中空地上

Let Me Describe the Rainstorm

Let me describe the rainstorm
It is nothing out of the ordinary
And in fact, it's already stopped
Last night, the rain beat down on broad leaves
Making the whole plane tree quiver

I've been through countless nights like this
Sometimes I'm still out in the street
Far away
I see lights in a window
Shining out into the darkness of the wind and rain
But it will take a long time
To walk over to the window

Last night I sat at home
My window shut
The lights turned off
The rain beat on the leaves
Then pinged onto the ground

This is spring rain, it will not make
The flowers wither and fall
In the world around, there's only
The rise and fall of joyful sobbing

Looks like a few more rains will have to fall
To express all the joy and sorrow from every heart
While real contentment comes
With a ray of sunlight
Shining in a woodland clearing

(1986)   45

记事

"有一件事也许应该告诉你
有关某人悲惨的结局……"
黑暗中他温和地笑着
亲切得像虚无人世的依靠
"可能是这样的，最后也无法确定
……"
"也许应该"、"可能"……
谨慎的言词如慈母手中的线
缝补一件百衲衣
那是一个无法缝补的故事
"可怜！"——打了一个结
可我心中的结试图穿过针鼻
树叶在暮色中油亮油亮的

Making a Note

"There's something I probably ought to tell you
So-and-so's come to a sad end . . ."
In the gloom, he smiles gently, lovingly
As if to say I can rely on him in this world of nothingness
"But the thing is, we could never be sure
. . ."
"We probably should" and "Possibly". . .
Earnest words like the thread in a foster mother's hand[*]
As she darns a monk's ragged robe
That's a story that can't be darned
"Poor man!" — The thread is knotted
But the knot in my heart tries to pass through the needle's eye
The tree leaves at dusk have an oily gleam

(2010)

* Proverbially, a foster mother shows more love than a birth mother.

对话

"你不会出家当和尚吧?
未来的一天我会去找你
你不会拒绝相认吧?"
女郎戏言挽留我, "还是别去吧!"

"我从没想过此去的前途
可我希望你来找我
如果这是我们相认的条件
那就在行走的路上建一座庙宇吧!"

白云的山腰, 青青的野草
山下走来了我的女郎
寺院以拒绝的姿势等待着
孤立的塔身也为之弯垂

"你知道在哪里能够找到我
那高耸的电视塔之东
与追求不朽的永生相比
实际上我只想要你。"

Dialogue

"You can't be leaving home to be a monk?!
I might come looking for you one day,
You'd not refuse to know me, would you?"
My lady chides me, smiling, "Don't go!"

"I never wondered where this road would take me,
But I hope you'll come looking for me
If acknowledging our friendship is conditional on this, then
Lets build a temple along the way!"

White-clouded mountains, green green grass
My lady comes up the mountain
Forbiddingly, the temple waits
And the lonely tower also bows

"You know where you can find me
East of the tall TV tower
Rather than seeking eternal life
I really just want you."

(1996)

消息

听说，她要走了
我在想，这对我
不意味任何东西
我们早在三年前就分手了
两年之内没再见面

我曾经狂热地爱过她
像一朵乱抖的火苗
现在，触摸这些往事的灰烬
我只感到指尖的温暖

当我们最后一次做爱
谁都不知道那是最后的
也许，这也不是最后的消息
最后的消息
已经来过了

News

I heard she was about to go
I'm thinking, that doesn't mean
Anything to me
We separated three years ago
And haven't seen each other for two.

I loved her desperately
Like a leaping tongue of flame
Now, if I touch the ashes of the past
I feel only warmth on my fingertips

The last time we made love
No one knew it was the last time.
This is really not the last news
The last news
Has already been and gone

(2000)

多么冷静

多么冷静
我有时也为之悲伤不已
一个人的远离
另一个的死
离开我们的两种方式
破坏我们感情生活的圆满性，一些
相对而言的歧途
是他们理解的归宿
只是，他们的名字遗落在我们中间
象这个春天必然的降临

So Dispassionate

So dispassionate
Sometimes it breaks my heart
Someone's distance
Another's death
Two ways of leaving us
Breaking apart the wholeness of our feelings
These deflections (comparatively speaking)
Are what they understand as going home
It's just that their names remain among us
Inevitable as this coming spring

(1996)

小姐

她的衣服从来不换。
我注意到，它是美丽的、肮脏的，
它是表姐的。
穷人无二件。

我注意到她身处的店堂、我们分属的阶级，
而性的微尘无理智地来往。
裸体的必要，比穿衣打扮更简单。
服饰比身体更令人羞愧，是可能的。

"小姐，你的穷
是空缺的财富。
你的空虚很实在，脸蛋儿被油腻衬托得更美。"

她的青春在搬动桌椅中度过一年。

Waitress

She never changes her clothes
I notice they're pretty, and dirty
They belong to her cousin
The poor don't have a change of clothes.

I notice the shop she's in, our class difference,
Dust motes of sex, irrational, move between us.
The need for nakedness, much simpler than dressing up.
A fine outfit is far more shaming than a body, possibly.

"Miss, your poverty
Is a wealth of vacancy.
Your emptiness quite material, your face made lovelier by contrast
            with the grease."

A year of her youth has passed in moving chairs and tables.

(1995)

夜航

和做服装生意的朋友一起旅行
他去进货，我参加一个文学会议
穿过夜晚的停机坪
我们走向那架童年的飞机

夜航，轻微的振动，有如摇篮
舷窗如同一块黑板
乡村的孩子涂抹星星
此刻我们在云层里或波涛下
空姐的微笑在一本画册上

叮零，并非上课的铃声
却降下柔和的阅读灯光
守纪律的学生将自己束在座椅上
分发食物，在更遥远的托儿所
稍后的寄宿生活里发出一片咀嚼之声

我的左耳疼痛，拒绝听讲的报应
波及脑袋，对政治的厌烦
而现在我们脱离了家长
自作主张，把前途交付给
一次危险的大人的游戏

让我们信任那物理课的高才生吧！
当年，那数学第一的同学为我们购买了保险
那身体轻盈犹如一张纸片的
正带着我们一起飞
后来做了我们忠实妻子的
还在我们高傲的俯视的下面

Night Flight*

I travelled with a friend in the clothing business
He to replenish his stock, and I to attend a literature conference
Walking across the tarmac at night
We approached the aeroplane of childhood

Night flight, a gentle rocking like a cradle
The window resembles a blackboard
Daubed with stars by village children
But now we are in the clouds or beneath the waves
A stewardess smiles from a glossy magazine

A ringing that is not a class bell
Yet a soft light shines down for reading
Obedient pupils are confined to their seats
And wait for their meal in a distant kindergarten
From boarding school there soon comes the sound of chewing

My left ear hurts; punishment for my refusal to listen
It has affected my brain, and made me sick of politics
But now that we are free of our parents
We have decided for ourselves to entrust the future
To a dangerous game for adults

Let's put our faith in the top physics student!
The one who came first in math that year bought insurance for us
The one whose body was as light as a sheet of paper
Is taking us flying now
Those who became our faithful wives
Are still subjected to our arrogant gaze

广州，炎热而陌生的异地
当年的同学迎接我
他是救护队员，今晚空闲
他和我们一起遗忘了那架飞机

Guangzhou, a hot and unfamiliar land
My former classmate has come to meet me
He is an ambulance man, off duty tonight
The three of us forget all about the plane

(1994)

---

* This series of five poems, beginning with "Night Flight," was written
after Han Dong's first visit to the then-brashly new city of Shenzhen.

横渡伶仃洋

对历史无知者横渡现实之伶仃洋
会使你晕船，在教课书以外
船尾的飞沫像白孔雀尾巴盛开
曹辉的午饭在他的腹中剧烈地翻滚
而一片白色的药片使我的心平静
中间状态的人在舱内昏睡
马达均匀的轰鸣外套古老的涛声
我们的船抚摸着伶仃洋、切开了伶仃洋
浸入其中，漫溢出的海水将两岸淹没
从荒凉的海上驶向未来的城
蛇口的楼影像照阳升起

从珠海到深圳
液体、柔软的路和移动的坟
有时候我们停在它的中间
不离一个地方更远或者更近
我们扩展了它但无法结束它
在鱼和水兽的家里
并无礼地立于那里的屋顶
我想到了死，但不是认真的
我的思想更倾向于两小时以后的宴会
有晕眩的印象都将被抹掉
只留下"叮零"洋敲击着碗盏

此外，我记得特殊环境中与
张文娟小姐唯一的私人接触——
给了她一枚白色的药片
但不是递与床头我妻子避孕的那枚
（"避晕"而非"避孕"）

Crossing the Lingdingyang, the Lonely Sea

For those ignorant of history, crossing the real-life Lonely Sea
Can make you seasick, outside of textbooks
At the stern, flying foam blooms like a peacock's tail
Cao Hui's lunch lurches violently in his belly
While a white pill calms me
Those in a middling state doze in the cabin
The engine's steady roar cloaks the ancient lapping of waves
Our boat is stroking the Lonely Sea, cuts it open
Becomes immersed, the brimming waters swamp both shores
From the desolate sea we sail to the coming city
The image of Shekou's buildings rises up like the morning sun

From Zhuhai to Shenzhen
A fluid, supple road and mobile tomb
Sometimes we stop in the middle
Not further from one place or nearer
We've expanded it but are unable to end it.
And at the home of fish and water beasts
We stand rudely on their roofs
I've thought about dying, but not that seriously
My thoughts lean more towards the banquet in two hours' time
Then, all impressions of queasiness will be erased
Leaving only the ding-a-ling sea knocking against the dishes

That aside, I remember the special circumstances in which
I had my only private contact with Miss Zhang Wenjuan —
I gave her a white pill
Not the contraceptive I pass my wife in bed
(A motion sickness pill, not "the" pill)

她接过，咽得也勉强
为她的胃正呼应着伶仃洋
不像我那么敏感，但有
更值得纠正的痛苦表情
她的红西服也蒙尘、起皱
并手握相当粗的铁管栏杆进入了底舱
哈，白茫茫的伶仃洋也不是爱情的海洋！

She took it, forced herself to swallow
For her stomach, which heaved along with the Lonely Sea
She seemed less sensitive than me, but wore
A pained expression much more in need of righting
And her red suit was dusty and crumpled
Then she gripped the crude iron handrail and went below to the cabin
Ha! The white expanse of the Lonely Sea is not the ocean of love!

(1994)

在深圳的路灯下……

在深圳的路灯下她有多么好听的名字
"流莺",有多么激动人心的买卖
身体的贸易
动物中唯有这一种拥有裸体
被剥出,像煮硬的鸡蛋,光滑
嫖妓者:我的堕落不是孤独的
我的罪恶也很轻微
她引领着一条地狱的河流
黑浪就来将我温柔地覆盖

那坐台女今晚和她的杯子在一起
杯子空了,她没有客人
杯子空了,就是空虚来临
她需要暗红色的美酒和另一种液体
让我来将它们注满,照顾她的生意
让我把我的钱花在罪恶上
不要阻挡,也不要害怕
灯光明亮,犹如一堆碎玻璃
让我将她领离大堂

我欣赏她编织的谎言
理解了她的冷淡
我尤其尊重她对金钱的要求
我敏感的心还注意到
厚重的脂粉下她的脸曾红过一次
我为凌乱的床铺而向她致歉
又为她懂得诗歌倍感惊讶
我和橡皮做爱,而她置身事外
真的,她从不对我说:我爱

Under the Streetlights of Shenzhen

In Shenzhen beneath the streetlights she has such a pretty name,
Wandering oriole, and a trade that stirs men's hearts
Body business
Of all animals only this type has a body
To be peeled naked, like a hard-boiled egg, smooth
Visiting a prostitute: my sin is not a solitary one
And my crime is only slight
She brings an infernal river
Black waves come and cover me tenderly

The woman sitting at the bar has her glass for company tonight
The glass is empty, she has no clients
Her glass is empty — an impending void
She needs dark red wine and another kind of liquid
Let me pour them out, and patronize her business
Let me spend my money on sin
Don't stop me, don't be afraid
The lights are bright, like piled-up glass
Let me take her away from the club

I enjoyed her lies
And understood her indifference
I especially respected her desire for money
I was sensitive enough to notice
When she blushed once beneath her heavy make-up
I apologized for the unmade bed
And was doubly astonished by her understanding of poetry
I made love to rubber, while she remained somewhere else
It's true, she never said to me: I love

(1994)

在深圳——致一帮朋友

在深圳，生活在朋友们中间
免于经济动物的伤害
没有足以儆戒他人的奋斗史
我只是来玩乐
请别提醒我太高兴了——难道这不应该？
请别认为我误解了深圳，而需要
领我去瞧打工妹拥挤的宿舍
我宁愿去发廊，见另一类姑娘
请别眼红我加速的堕落
既不是来奋斗，也不试图理解
让我生活在灯红酒绿的表面
好像一条鱼，误认玻璃为海洋
请别对我讲责任，讲底层的欲望
要讲就讲强盗和小偷
在福田，一位农妇剪断了丈夫的阴茎
警察和他的同事在黎明前的草丛中捉"青蛙"
要讲就讲好玩的，可乐的
讲我在深圳，如何浮光掠影和走马观花
甚至走遍了五十六个民族，在地图状的民俗村
好玩的和可乐的，在小丁的宿舍
就像走进了他心灵的房间
每一件物品都代表他的一个癖好
每一种混乱都另有深意
他拒绝恋爱中的女人进入，其危险
就是粉拳砸在小腰上，伤筋动骨，与性命有碍
而妓女们的蜜蜂飞来飞去
劳动采蜜于小丁的钱包
我要讲，南国电影院门前的风景
远胜于野生动物园

In Shenzhen, to a Group of Friends

In Shenzhen, living among friends
Free from the harm inflicted by the economy beast
No story of struggle to serve as a lesson to others
I just came to enjoy myself
Don't tell me I'm having too much fun — why shouldn't I?
Don't think I've misunderstood Shenzhen, and must
Be taken to inspect the cramped dorms of the migrant worker girls
I'd rather go to a "salon," to see another kind of girl
Don't lament my slide into debauchery
I didn't come to struggle, or to try to understand
Let me live on a streetlight-red and beery-green surface
Like a fish, mistaking glass for the sea
Don't talk to me about responsibility or base desires
If you want to talk, talk about robbers and thieves
In Futian, a peasant woman chopped off her husband's penis
The cops and his workmates caught the "frog" in the pre-dawn thickets
If you want to talk, talk of fun and fizz,
Of me in Shenzhen, how I'm skimming the surface of life
And even strayed through fifty-six nationalities in a map-shaped folk village
It was fun and fizz in Xiao Ding's hostel
Like walking into a room in his soul
Every thing represents one of his pursuits
Each bit of mess has another meaning
He keeps his lady-love out, in case
Her little fists pummel his back and break his bones and she interferes in his life
Yet the honey-bee whores fly in and out
Labouring to find honey in Xiao Ding's wallet.
I want to talk about the scene in front of Southern Cinema
Beats the zoo any day

三百只雄兽延长了这里的春天
而在十年未见的陈寅家里
我不认识那无故多出的七十斤！
肥胖稳定了他钟摆般的心脏
而我喜欢了胖人的安详
还有那酷似耶稣的朋友，多么瘦
他的焦虑就像熏鱼
还要去洪湖公园烤肉、冒油
还爱上了风鸡肌肉的美好口味
我参观了他的工厂，并和打工仔们讨论：
一个精瘦的老板已属不易
一个老板耶稣更是世所罕见
所有的朋友都去桑拿间相见
在温柔水雾之乡，按摩室的床（船）
幸福地迷航
今晚的仙湖公园内乐声悠扬
小小的餐厅矗立在草地上
我们在二楼吃穿山甲
去一楼木棉树的根部呕吐
凉气正从湖上上来，漫过
大人物的手植的树
我的一泡带体温的小便为其施肥
我的，小丁、陈寅和耶稣的，还有曹旭、李潮的
我们围成一圈，将泥地淋湿
希望获得好运

Three hundred tomcats prolonging springtime
While at the home of Chen Yin, not seen for ten years
I don't recognise those extra seventy pounds
Fat has steadied his pendulum-like heart
I like the fat man's gravitas
Then there's another friend, a sort of cool Jesus, dead skinny
His anxiety is just like smoked fish
He's off to Honghu Park for a BBQ where he gleams with sweat
And adores the marvellous taste of wind-dried chicken
I visit his factory, and talk to the migrant worker kids:
A skinny boss is hard enough to come by
But a Jesus boss is an even rarer bird
My friends all meet at the sauna
In the realm of warm vapour, on the beds (the boat) of the massage room
We're happily adrift
At the Xianhu Park this evening the music rises and falls
A tiny cafe looms on a patch of grass
We eat armadillo upstairs
We go downstairs to hawk and spit on the cotton tree roots
Cool air rises from the lake and wafts towards us
I piss a body-warm stream to fertilize
The tree personally planted by some VIP
There's my piss, Xiao Ding's, Chen Yin's and Jesus's, and Cao Xu's and Li Chao's
We stand in a circle, soaking the mud
Hoping we'll get lucky

(1994)

归来

我回来了，从深圳到南京
白天还没有结束
不能说我不理解时间
不能说，这样幼稚的话
——既然我已预备了棉衣
穿着它到家
只是，夜晚降临，那南方的阳光在我的体内
仍未熄灭

我去拍击朋友家的门
把他们唤到寒冷的街上来
我愚蠢地说：零点刚过，在深圳
一切不过刚刚开始！
没有人和我争辩，他们
习惯于沉默
在夫妻的床上延长夫妻的生活
或背靠（烤）着背，互相取暖

（其后的一个月里
我满怀背叛的愿望
我欢呼"我已变样！"
然而不过是生物钟的紊乱
时差或作息表的改变
一只神秘的手于暗中
慢慢调整）

我更深地陷入往昔
就像从空中落下，继续
钻入泥土。冬天像一支大军深入

Return

I returned from Shenzhen to Nanjing
There was still some daylight left
It wasn't that I didn't understand time
You couldn't say anything so naive
Having taken a padded jacket with me
I put it on when I went back home
And yet, as the evening approached
My body retained the southern sunlight
Still unextinguished

I went knocking at my friends' doors
And called them out into the icy streets
I said stupidly: It's after midnight, in Shenzhen
Everything is just starting!
No one argued with me, being
Used to silence
They got on with their lives in double beds as husband and wife
Or back to back, drawing warmth from each other

(For a month afterwards I was full of rebellious hopes and desires
And cried joyfully: "I have changed!"
But it was only a disturbance of my biological clock
The difference in time zones, or the changes in my schedule
There was a mysterious and unseen hand slowly adjusting
 In the darkness)

Now I am sinking deeper into the past
As though falling from the sky, continuing
My plunge into the earth.
Winter is settling into its siege

围困。寒冷甚至使金属收缩
而在南方，最柔软的就最美好地开放
像花朵，和生殖器官
淫荡依赖于海上和贸易的熏风

我回到了南京
起居在冰雪和霜冻附近
像那些远古的圣人，在西亚、帕米尔
在雪峰和冰川的附近
热带是不会产生圣人的。我理解了
耶稣不是一个黑人

我回来了，回到了南京
继续某种中间生活
在太阳和冰雪之间，处于
房间阴冷的影子里
偶尔出入于歌厅
那温暖的洞穴
远离永恒或刺激的一瞬
我像所有平庸而痛苦的存在
我就是

Like a great army.
Even metals contract in the cold
But in the south, the softest things open up in the finest way
Like flowers and their sexual organs
Licentiousness depends on warm ocean breezes and the trade winds

Now I'm back in Nanjing
Living near ice, snow and frost
Like the saints of ancient times in the Pamir mountains of Central Asia
Close to snow-capped peaks and glaciers
The tropics can produce no saints.
I know very well
That Jesus was not a black man

Now I'm back, back in Nanjing
Getting on with a middling kind of life
Between sun and ice, I inhabit
The cold shadows of my room
Occasionally visiting a nightclub
That warm cave
Where I am far from eternity or a moment of excitement
I'm like any commonplace and painful existence
That's all I am

(1994)

爱情生活

有可能
就尽量做爱
不做爱
也要抱着
要互相说话
彼此看着
不能走神
你在想什么
我在想你
生气的时候
不拿正眼看你
也要拿白眼看你
不说话的时候
也要在心里骂你

要保持
清醒的状态
不要睡过去
睡觉是各自的事情
要抱着睡
握着睡
在里面睡
至少也要
手拉着手
像在过一条
车流飞奔
凶险万状的
马路

Love Life

If you can
Make love as much as possible
If you don't make love
You can still embrace
Talk to each other
Looking at each other
Don't let your thoughts stray
Whatever you're thinking of
I'm thinking of you
Even when I'm angry
And can't look you in the eye
I'll still glare at you
When we're not talking
I'll still curse you silently

We should stay
Clear-headed
Not go to sleep
Sleeping is an individual matter
We should sleep in each other's arms
Holding onto each other
Inside each other
At least we should
Hold hands
As if we were crossing
A highway
Fraught with hazards
With cars whizzing by

(2001)

冬天的荒唐景色

这是冬天荒唐的景色
这是中国的罗马大街
太阳的钥匙圈还别在腰上
霞光已打开了白天的门

这是炭条画出的树枝
被再一次烧成了炭条
这是雪地赠与的白纸
还是画上雪地

瞧，汽车在表达个性
商店在拍卖自己
梧桐播撒黄叶，一个杨村人
日夜思念着巴黎

垃圾上升起狼烟
大厦雾霭般飘移
而人与兽，在争夺
本属于兽的毛皮

这是南方的北方寒冬
这是毛巾变硬的室内
这并不是电脑病毒的冬眠期
不过是思之花萎缩的几日

Absurd Winter Scene

This is an absurd winter scene
This is China's Roman road
The sun's keyring still hangs at the waist
The dawn light opens the door to day

This is a tree branch drawn in charcoal
Then burned once again into a stick of charcoal
This is white paper bestowed by the snowy ground
Lets draw a snowy ground on it

Look, the car expresses individuality
The shop is selling itself off
The plane tree spreads its yellow leaves, someone in Willow Village
Dreams of Paris day and night

Smoke signals rise from the rubbish
Tower blocks drift by like a mist
While humans and beasts fight over
Furs which properly belong to the beasts

This is the South's Northern winter cold
This is an indoors where the scarf grows stiff
This is not hibernation time for computer viruses
But it is a few days when the flowers of thought shrivel

(1993)

疼

她疼得死去活来
从外表看
她的身体静静的
她从香一直疼到臭
用手遮着脸
从妩媚动人
一直疼到没脸见人
喂，好点吗
对别人的关心询问
不作反应
她从能言善辩疼到了
哑口无言
当我们掰开她的手
帮助她起立
就从柔然顺从的少女
疼到了僵硬固执的尸体

Pain

Pain has driven her to the brink
To all appearances
Her body lies inert
Pain makes her smell foul
She hides her face behind her hands
This once charming girl is
Effaced by pain
Is it a bit better now?
No response
To others' concerned questions
Pain has reduced her fluency with words
To dumb silence
When we pry away her hands to help her stand
Pain gives this once sweet compliant girl
The stubborn rigidity of a corpse

(2001)

成长的错误

只一年。一年前
无法预测这些变化
你脱离孩子的形体
像一次成功
阳光下缩小瞳孔
一些雄性物质绕着你飞
一年，分分秒秒都出了差错
你的头发不再是光滑的布匹
我从未看出你是个美人
你我行我素，走上美人之途
坚持月光下的进军
再灿烂的东西也经不住
这冷静的光辉

正好一年，太阳改造一个孩子
像最后时刻的淬火
为了另一批孩子的诞生
我走下台阶，记着你的幼稚体态
感到成长是一个错误
其次是时间

Growing Up Is a Mistake

Just one year. A year ago
No one could foresee these changes
You left behind your childish form,
As if this was a great success.
Your pupils contract in the sun
Male matter swirls around you
One year, mistakes made every minute, every second
Your hair no longer a glossy curtain
I hadn't seen you as a beauty
You go your own way, walking a beauty's road
Marching, determined, by the light of the moon
More splendid things cannot penetrate
The coolness of your brilliance

In just one year the sun has transformed a child
Like the last flicker of a flame
So that another batch of children can be born
I walk down the steps, remembering your childish figure
I think that growing up is a mistake
Time comes next

(2000)

日子

日子是空的
一些人住在里面
男人和女人
就像在车厢里偶然相遇
就像日子和日子那样亲密无间

日子摇晃着我们
抱得更紧些吧
到站下车，热泪挥洒
一只蝴蝶飞进来
穿梭无碍

The Days of Our Lives

The days are empty
Some people live in them
Men and women
Meeting by chance, as on a train
Joined as intimately as one day and the next

Life rocks and shakes us
Hold me tighter!
Get off at the station, shed hot tears
A butterfly flits in
Shuttling back and forth, unfettered flight

(2003)

温柔的部分

我有过寂寞的乡村生活
它形成了我生活中温柔的部分
每当厌倦的情绪来临
就会有一阵风为我解脱
至少我不那么无知
我知道粮食的由来
你看我怎样把清贫的日子过到底
并能从中体会到快乐
而早出晚归的习惯
捡起来还会象锄头那样顺手
只是我再也不能收获些什么
不能重复其中每一个细小的动作
这里永远怀有某种真实的悲哀
就象农民痛哭自己的庄稼

The Softer Part

I have led a lonely country life
It formed the softer part of my character
Whenever a mood of weariness descends on me
There comes a liberating breeze
At least I am not so ignorant
I know where our food comes from
See how I endured the days of poverty to the end
But could still find happiness in them
And the habit of going out early and returning late
In reverting to it I am still as deft as with the hoe
It's just that I can no longer harvest anything
Can no longer rehearse each of those trivial actions
Here I am always haunted by a genuine anguish
Just like a peasant who weeps bitterly for his crops

(1985)

木工

木工车间里工人们躺在刨花里干活
没有门，没有窗，也没有墙
只有芦席围起三面的金色工棚
只有阳光、刨花和木料和
已雕刻成型的各类农具的柄
没有门，没有窗，没有桌凳和门槛
没有床。是木工取消了木工
刨花掩盖了泥土

Wood Work

The wood workers lie at work in the sawdust
Their workshop has no door, no windows and no walls.
Just a shack with blonde rush matting on three sides.
Just sunlight, sawdust, wood and
The shaped hafts of every kind of farm tool
No door, no windows, benches or doorsill
No lathe. This wood work has done away with wood work
Sawdust has covered up the mud floor

(1993)

夏日窗口

七点以后
天色依然很亮
一群老太太
在院子里做操
转动腰身
挥舞胳膊
乐感因人而异

窗口的绿叶间
我看见她们在下面
树叶随风轻颤
她们动了又动
像一些果子
东一个西一个

Summertime Window

After seven o'clock
There's still brightness in the sky
A cluster of old women
Exercise in the courtyard
Bending and stretching
Waving their arms
All moving to a different beat

I see them downstairs
Between the leaves at my window
Trembling in the breeze
The women bounce up and down
Like fruit on a tree
Turning this way and that

(2001)

我们坐在街上

我们坐在街上
店铺的灯光已经熄灭了
天色将明未明之际
青色的帷幕下面
对面的黑影僵硬

一年没见
但已经无话可说
火热的锅冷了
酒寒像心情
开始的清晨在熬夜的人看来
像惨淡的结局

We Sat on the Street

We sat on the street
The shop lights were switched off
A crack of dawn in the night sky
The shadow opposite was rigid
Beneath the blue-black curtain

We hadn't seen each other for a year
But there was nothing left to say
The pot had gone off the boil
Liquor chills like feelings cool
If you've been up all night, the start of a new day
Is like a dreary ending

(2003)

在瓷砖贴面的光明中

在瓷砖贴面的光明中沉思
有时痛快淋漓
有时劳而无功
带着手纸擦揩的奇妙感觉
投身于司空见惯的百态人生

我曾在寺院的厕所里亲眼所见
一位僧人，撩开布袍
空通一声
拉得如此气宇轩昂
如此爽利
已达免纸水平

想起了我那可怜的老外公
蹲在红漆马桶上挣命
十趾抓地，面如猪肝
老外婆当年生小孩
恐怕也没有这么艰难

In White-tiled Brightness

In white-tiled brightness I'm sunk in thought
Sometimes there's a merry splashing
Sometimes it's all striving no gain
The miraculous comfort of paper on bum
Those tiles are devoted to serving all comers
They've seen it all

I once saw this in a temple toilet:
A monk, hitching up his robes
"Ker-plunk" . . .
He shat with such easy dignity
With such efficiency
Having reached a higher plane, he had no need to wipe

I thought of poor granddad
Squatted, straining, over the red-painted bucket
Curled toes gripping, face pig-liver purple with effort
I bet my Gran never suffered half as much
When she gave birth to my mum

(2006)

一些人不爱说话

一些人不爱说话
既不是哑巴，也不内向
只说必要的话
只是礼节
只浮在说话的上面
一生就将这样过去
寥寥数语即可概括
一些人活着就像墓志铭
漫长但言词简短
像墓碑那样伫立着
与我们冷静相对

Some People Don't Like to Talk

Some people don't like to talk
They're not dumb or introverted
They only speak when necessary
Just courtesies
Just floating on the surface of talk
They spend their whole lives like that
It can be summed up very briefly
The way some people live is like an epitaph
Long years but the words are short and simple
Upright as tombstones
They stand soberly before us

(2004)

起雾了

起雾了，或者是烟尘
或者是雾和烟的混合物
没有谁惊讶于这一点

可以直视太阳，在灰白的云层中
像月亮一样飘动
没有谁惊讶于这一点

我的这个上午和其它的上午一样
我的昨天几乎等于明天
没有谁惊讶于这一点

即使是晴朗的日子我也看不清沿途的花和树
即使看清了，也记不住
即使记住了，也写不出

如果我不惊讶于这一点
就没有人惊讶于这一点

敷衍生活比敷衍一件事容易多了
应付世界也比应付一个人容易多了
增长了即时反应，丧失了全知全能

在一片弥漫的浓雾中我机警地躲避着来往的车辆
穿越这座城

It's Foggy

It's foggy, or smoky
Or perhaps it's smog
No one's surprised by that

You can look straight into the sun, floating
Like the moon in ashen clouds
No one's surprised by that

This morning for me is just like other mornings
Yesterday and tomorrow are pretty much the same
No one's surprised by that

Even on a clear day, I don't see roadside flowers and trees clearly
Even if I see them, I don't remember them
Even if I remember them, I can't write about them

If I'm not surprised by that, then
No one else'll be surprised by that

A lot easier to muddle through life than to muddle through one thing
A lot easier to cope with the world than with one person
More knee-jerk reactions mean fewer prescient actions

I cut through this city blanketed in thick fog
Cannily avoiding the traffic

(2009)

这些年

这些年，我过得不错
只是爱，不再恋爱
只是睡，不再和女人睡
只是写，不再诗歌
我经常骂人，但不翻脸
经常在南京，偶尔也去
外地走走
我仍然活着，但不想长寿

这些年，我缺钱，但不想挣钱
缺觉，但不吃安定
缺肉，但不吃鸡腿
头秃了，就让它秃着吧
牙蛀空了，就让它空着吧
剩下的已经够用
胡子白了，下面的胡子也白了
眉毛长了，鼻毛也长了

这些年，我去过一次上海
但不觉得上海的变化很大
去过一次草原，也不觉得
天人合一
我读书，只读一本，但读了七遍
听音乐，只听一张CD，每天都听
字和词不再折磨我
我也不再折磨语言

这些年，一个朋友死了
但我觉得他仍然活着
一个朋友已迈入不朽

These Past Few Years

I've not done badly these past few years
Except that I love but have no more love affairs
And sleep, but not with women anymore
And though I write, there's no more poetry
I'm often surly, but don't fall out with anyone
I'm usually in Nanjing, though there's an off-chance
I might go out of town on trips
I'm alive, but not looking forward to old age

These past few years, I've been short of money but have no desire to earn
I'm short of sleep, but not on tranqs
Short of meat, but I don't eat chicken legs
I'm going bald — hey, let the hairs fall out
I'm losing teeth — well, so be it
I can get by with the ones I've got left
My beard's gone grey — and so's my "beard" down there
Long hairs grow from my eyebrows, and out of my nostrils

These past few years, I've been to Shanghai once
But I didn't see those "great changes"
I've been once to the grasslands, but I didn't feel
"At one with nature"
I've read books — or rather one book, seven times
Listened to music, just one CD, the same one every day
Words don't torment me any more
And I don't torment language either

These past few years, a friend has died
But it still feels like he's alive
Another's shot to fame

那就拜拜，就此别过
我仍然是韩东，但人称老韩
老韩身体健康，每周爬山
既不极目远眺，也不野合
就这么从半山腰下来了

So it's bye-bye. Lets part right here
I'm still Han Dong but now they call me "old man"
This old man's still hale, goes climbing every week
Though he doesn't gaze from the hilltop, or have sex outdoors anymore
And half-way up the hill, he's on his way down again

(2002)

Translator Acknowledgments

Translated by Nicky Harman:
Green Tree, Red Fruit; A Loud Noise; A Phone Call from Dalian; The Worker's Hand; The Chicken Seller; The Train; Let Me Describe the Rainstorm; Making a Note; Dialogue; News; So Dispassionate; Waitress; Crossing the Lingdingyang, the Lonely Sea; In Shenzhen, to a Group of Friends; Love Life; Absurd Winter Scene; Pain; Growing Up Is a Mistake; The Days of Our Lives; Wood Work; Summertime Window; We Sat on the Street; In White-tiled Brightness; Some People Don't Like to Talk; It's Foggy; These Past Few Years

Translated by Maghiel van Crevel:
Someone in a Riot of Stones; There Is a Darkness; Of the Wild Goose Pagoda; Mountain People; So You've Seen the Sea; A and B

Translated by Yu Yan Chen:
Visiting Shandong; A Calm; Round Jade; Rain; Gregorian Chant; Elevator Door Etc.

Translated by Naikan Tao and Tony Prince:
Night Flight; Under the Streetlights of Shenzhen; Return; The Softer Part

Translated by Michael Day:
I Hear Cups; Your Hand

Translator Biographies

NICKY HARMAN has been translating for twelve years. Her work includes *Gold Mountain Blues* 《金山》 by Zhang Ling (2011), *Flowers of War* by Yan Geling (2012) and Han Dong's *Banished!* 《扎根》 (2009), which was longlisted for the Man Asian Literary Prize. She is currently working on *A New Development Model and China's Future* 《新发展方式与中国的未来》 by Deng Yingtao, and translates regularly for *Chutzpah* literary magazine. She has been Translator-in-Residence in a London arts centre and is active on the Chinese-to-English translators' website, Paper Republic (paper-republic.org).

MAGHIEL VAN CREVEL is Professor of Chinese Language & Literature at Leiden University, and an internationally recognized expert on modern Chinese poetry. He has published extensively in English, Dutch and Chinese, for specialist and general audiences. His scholarly books include *Language Shattered: Contemporary Chinese Poetry and Duoduo* (1996) and *Chinese Poetry in Times of Mind, Mayhem and Money* (2008).

YU YAN CHEN is a poet, interpreter and translator. She was born in a fishing village in China but grew up in New York City. Enchanted by the traveler's tales her grandfather told, she set sail to seek her own adventures. Her debut poetry collection *Small Hours* was published by NYQ Books in 2011. She lives in Brooklyn.

NAIKAN TAO is a literary translator and critic working on Chinese and English literatures. He has published, with Tony Prince, *Eight Contemporary Chinese Poets* (Wild Peony) and with Simon Patton *Starve the Poet: Selected Poems of Yi Sha* (Bloodaxe), and is the author of *Pangde yu Zhongguo wenhua* (*Ezra Pound and Chinese Culture*; Capital Normal University Press) and of several essays on Chinese poetry and on Chinese and Western literary relations. He now teaches at the University of Canberra.

After completing a PhD thesis in modern Chinese literature at the University of Sydney, TONY PRINCE spent three years teaching at the College of Chinese Culture (now the Chinese Culture University) in Taiwan. After a further two years in Japan, he returned to the University of Sydney in 1977, where he taught courses in Chinese language, literature and thought until his retirement in 2000. He has published material on Huayen Buddhism and Chinese poetry.

MICHAEL DAY was hired as an assistant professor of literature at National University in La Jolla, CA, in January 2007. In October 2005, he completed his doctorate under the supervision of Maghiel van Crevel at the University of Leiden on the subject of the development of avant-garde poetry in Sichuan province during the 1980s. He has published numerous English language translations of Chinese poetry, fiction, and prose, as well as articles on Chinese poetry and politics.

JINTIAN SERIES OF CONTEMPORARY LITERATURE

In Print

Flash Cards
Yu Jian
Translated by Wang Ping & Ron Padgett

The Changing Room
Zhai Yongming
Translated by Andrea Lingenfelter

Doubled Shadows
Ouyang Jianghe
Translated by Austin Woerner

Forthcoming

Wind Says
Bai Hua
Translated by Fiona Sze Lorraine